Between Selves

Poems

Diana Cole

ISBN: 978-81-962026-9-9

First Edition: 2023
Rs. 200/-

Cyberwit.net
HIG 45 Kaushambi Kunj, Kalindipuram
Allahabad - 211011 (U.P.) India
http://www.cyberwit.net
Tel: +(91) 9415091004
E-mail: info@cyberwit.net

Printed at VCORE.

Acknowledgments

Many thanks to the publications in which these poems first appeared, sometimes in earlier versions and with different titles:

Avocet: "Afternoon Coronas," "A Day Like No Other," *Blueline*: "Loosestrife"; *Blue Unicorn*: "Reckoning"; *The Comstock Review:* "Sitting for Diego Rivera"; *Damselfly Press*: "Packing"; *Ibbetson:* "My Father's Annual Stint in the National Guard"; *Main Street Rag:* "Split Infinity"; *Muddy River Review:* "Nik Wallenda Walks a Wire across Niagara Falls"; *Ocean State Poets Anthology: Giving Voice/2020:* "Contraction"; *Off the Coast*: "Food on the Table"; *Poeming Pigeon*: "On the Scent of a Tune"; *San Pedro River Review*: "That Otherwise Might Be"; *Slipstream:* "The Day My Mother Dies"; *Songs By Heart: Poems by Diana Cole* (Iris Press 2018): "Pastorales Tahitiennes," "The Crow"; *Spillway*: "Doing the Puzzle," "Muse"; *Slipstream*: "The Day My Mother Died"; *The Aurorean*: "Breakfast in Barrington"; *The Ekphrastic Review:* "Looking Hard at What You See"; *The Wickford Art /Poetry Exhibition Catalogue*: "What You Make of It"; *Touch: Journal of Healing*: "Late Summer," "Dressing."

Between selves is a place of breaking down, reassembling and becoming. These poems are largely a story of my own life and I am indebted to all the people who crossed my path and influenced these stories — the tragedies and comedies, the romances and unsolved mysteries. I especially would like to pay tribute to my parents, Polly and Charlie Cole whose love and loyalty to each other and to me never wavered.

On the cover is the beautiful image, Altered Self, which I owe to the talent and generosity of Felicia Touhey, a fellow Rhode Island artist. I am grateful as well for two poetry groups that have helped review and improve these poems: The Poetry Loft and the Black Oak Poets. Your friendship, insights and support have been invaluable. I'd also like to recognize April Ossman, whose editorial expertise helped these poems find their best place in the manuscript to create the evolution of self I wanted to convey.

Contents

I

The Muse 11
Contraction 12
Off to Work 14
Doing the Puzzle 15
Dressing 16
Tomboy 17
Convenience 18
Mental Status Exam 19
Love is a Game 20
The Goldfinch 21
Split Infinity 23
The Crow 24

II

What She Sees Through 27
I Tell You to Go 28
A Marriage in Six Albums 30
Self-Discipline 32
Food on the Table 33
At the Nursing Home 34
The Secret 35
Otherwise 36
White Peony 37
Pantomime 38
Open Mic Night 39

III

It's Been a Clear Day 43
The Night Passes Quickly 44

The Day My Father Died 45
Late Summer 46
I Have the Will to Do So 47
My Dead Father Writes to My Dying Mother 48
My Father's Annual Stint in the National Guard 49
Fireworks 50
Sitting for Diego Rivera 51
You were so mad at me 53

IV

Let Me Try to Understand 57
The Road Was Narrow 61
Invictus Inverted 62
Pastorales Tahitiennes 64
Packing 65
On the Scent of a Tune 66
The Lure 68
Reckoning 70
Miniature Persimmon, Dark Orange 71
Letter to Myself Unremembered 72

V

Between Selves 75
The Day My Mother Dies 77
I Own This 78
Looking Hard at What You See 79
Closure 81
A Day Like No Other 82
Refrain 84
Nik Wallenda Walks a Wire across Niagara Falls 85
What You Make of It 87

What I've wrung out of love
is not one steady course

but a dozen starts,
a dozen frangible ends

I

The Muse

Strike the viol, touch the lute
—Nahum Tate

The moth with folded wings
motionless on the window sill
camouflaged among ordinary things,

watches the flame burning
from the lamp until
the moth with folded wings

twitches with the asking
the why of standing still
camouflaged among ordinary things,

when light but briefly clings
to the wick, the ink to the quill.
The moth with folded wings

lifts off the ledge of being
loath, thrashes at the gilt,
camouflaged among ordinary things,

willing to risk everything
for sake of light—to kill
itself, the moth with folded wings,
camouflaged among ordinary things.

Contraction

Why favor the heart as love's logo,
    this fist of muscle,
    machine of the status quo,
    motor of the go-go-go.

It didn't stop when I felt it should.

How the word contrives to heave and sigh,
    soften to kindness,
    harden to hate,
    clichéd to death.

It didn't break when I said it would.

Why favor the heart as love's logo,
    its piffling, 11-ounce weight,
    its chambered cells,
    its one-way doors.

It didn't skip a beat when my father died.

How the shape survives,
    two halves joined,
    pressed against lace,
    promising the only, the endless.

A heart has no allegiance.

It metes out a random ration
to panhandler,
baron,
sinner or saint.

A heart has no preference,
motoring impoverished blood
along with the enriched.
It beats on and on,

toward one momentous spasm
or exhausted spurt.

Off to Work

Every day a starched white shirt
still creased, stiff barrel cuffs
buttoned, two loops of his tie
before the knot drawn tight, his hug,
tweed scratching my cheek,

then my father was out the door,
face half shadowed by the fedora
with the brown felt rim, the ribbon's
grosgrain sheen almost spectral,
his blue Ford disappearing.

Every evening, home at five,
tie loosened, jacket off,
shirt pliant and subdued,
graphite smudges on rolled up sleeves,
his hand out

for the first beer,
or if Friday, a three-olive martini.
Voices back and forth,
exchanging stories, laughing,
as if the day was just beginning.

Doing the Puzzle

I am snug with what seems perfect,
cardboard cutouts,
a picture of what love should be.

I insist myself
into an available coupling.

Although I work the puzzle for years,
a tree branch impales
the lake's glazed surface

and I can't find the last piece
of the yellow house.

Dressing

To begin, my mother must bend slowly:
    a foot lifts, passes into the rolled nylon.
Hands crab up the leg, easing fine mesh
    over each knee. She unbends,
draws the fabric over her hips,
    exhaling in spurts of exertion.
        As the chair catches her fall,
            it knocks out a sigh.

There was a time she stood on one leg
to add red paint to a carousel horse.
A time her hands wet a thread,
caught the eye in one try.
A time they flexed stems,
coaxed Camellias into an ikebana vase.

Now, thumb and forefinger fumble
    each disc through its buttonhole,
to rest, anchored by a shred.
    All this before 9 AM.
To sit, to read, even just to nap,
    knowing her skirt is smooth,
        stockings straight, laces tied,
            earrings, lipstick, rouge.

Tomboy

My father mowed even strips,
a gentle fluttering
of the reel. He curbed
the wild, ever-growing grass,
and my unruly ways.

Some days he'd dab my chin
with a beard of Barbasol,
before mounding his face with white.
As black whiskers disgraced the sink,
I washed them down.

If my father hadn't said:
It would have been nice
to have a boy finally,
when my mother miscarried.
If I hadn't overheard.

I should have been a boy.
Together we would have set up
that train set, sailed Boston Harbor,
nailed together a go-kart,
watched football.

One winter, he built a snow slide
over the swing set—slick
enough to send my sled flying
into a soft white drift,
a safe landing for a girl.

Convenience

The anemone spends days
soaking in water.
Waits.
With each fish, a tingle,
tentacle shudder.
The kill.

Only the clown fish,
her turquoise skirt,
flittering yellow scarves,
escapes his poison.
Indifferent
the kiss.

He harbors her,
she keeps house,
isopods and zooplankton
sucked down her gullet.
They are companionable,
holding off intruders.
Complacent.

Above, a brilliant blue ceiling.
Below, flickering sea grass,
pink stars trailing.

Mental Status Exam

What comes after Sunday and Monday?
Wednesday, my mother says.

How small she looks,
head down, watching her hands.

Hair like silk with glimpses of scalp.
She still makes sense of wrong.

Please count from 10 backwards.
The numbers don't add up.

Her voice weakens and breaks,
scattered pearls, value unknown.

Here's a clock, fill in the face.
And she does! A perfect circle of time

from her childhood sketchbook,
a gesture of hand, almost robotic.

Remember these words: cat, shoe, teapot.
My mother nods.

Oh, what will words undo?
Words she taught me in songs.

She can define *luster* and *raspy.*
Knows *hyacinths* are flowers.

Yet loses *shoe* and *teapot.*
Even the cat jumps off her lap.

Love is a Game

that wants no winner. Two
people share a length of string.

Know to loop and cross.
Not to pull too tight.

Each takes a turn. I
swap a diamond for a cradle.

You make a cat's eye
from a candle.

Too lax and we might
slip the running noose.

Who will take up the slack?
Who will cast off first?

A game is done when love
has nothing more to lose.

The Goldfinch

—after Carel Fabritius

A sleight of hand,
a master stroke,
to capture a bird
in captivity.
The fine chain allows
but a hop
from one brass bar
to one below.
A cold landing,
no sway of twig.
Wings flail and lift
a span of ten
short inches; then
the yank, defeat.
How the family loves
to hear her sing!

To guild that feather gold,
did the artist work
from memory or wait
for one still moment
the bird would fold its wing
to be a pretty thing?
Did the artist train
his eye to shade
each link of chain,
locking o to o to o

like tiny gasps
    along its length?
Such nimble marks
    this artist makes.
And yet for me
    she will not sing.

The painting asks I touch
    the racing pulse,
red mask ringing
    uneasy eyes,
stubby beak prying open
    the box to feed.
It asks I read and learn
    the bird could draw
a thimble-full of water
    from a well. All this,
because she cannot help
    a merry song.
It fills her lungs—and all
    lean in to hear.
And yet for me, for me
    she will not sing.

Split Infinity

We meet mornings
over eggs. *Over*
easy, I say.

    It's over,
    too hard to say.

The yolk can't be broken.
We stab at it repeatedly.

The tines are bent,
I say, all I dare
to say.

We ask for refill after refill
of house blend.

    I want something stronger.

You say, *I'll take half & half.*

I say, *I'll take it black.*

The Crow

Yes, I have something to say, but saying it
is like striking a wet match. Inside I'm raw
from mouthing artifice and spasm wit
while at my hand jabs the hungry crow.

Strings stiffen, thinking stretched on frets,
fingers plunking out haphazard tunes,
double meanings forged and faked to death,
as crickets shrill awake the hunter's moon.

But what thrill the rubbing wings, calling it
over noisy critics in the grass. I'll wring
my knuckles white. I'll write till sky is lit,
advancing over stone walls singing—

and I have something to feed the crow,
something mineral-rich, something I didn't know.

II

What She Sees Through

She looks off not answering.
We lean in with searchlights
and sirens: *Mom, Mom?*
Boo!, she says with her half smile,
her timing brilliant.

*

What's happening to me?
I feel different.
She asks this of the aide, not me.
To my question, she says she's fine.
A mother has answers.

*

Propped, eyes half-closed,
she bolts straight up, staring through
what I see as a solid wall.
Silent as an owl into the dark,
she has flown from me.

I Tell You to Go

You stand on the lower step,
grip the railing. I slump
on the landing, glad you're home.

It is 5 am, our son sleeping upstairs.
We need to talk, you say,
sweat on your upper lip.

In the half-light of that morning,
bats return to our attic
to feed their young.

The dull skirr of their wings
says it all—this will be your last trip home.
You don't know my heart

hangs upside down, rocking itself sick.
And you don't know our son
awake is listening.

What a fine idea it seemed,
this open marriage thing; yes, my idea,
a one-time fling, to pick clean

the evening sky of boredom.
This was the year we tried and failed
to rid the house of bats. The year

I woke to tingling on my arm,
chased the bat out the window,
no way to test if it was rabid.

So, on that stairway at 5 am,
I tell you to go, as if it will ease
the trouble of caring.

Later, I must take each
painful injection to stay alive,
knowing its necessity.

A Marriage in Six Albums

Black and white photographs tucked into corners,
captions on pasted strips, in strike-on type.

> August 1936: Acadia honeymoon cottage.
> My mother leans on a railing, her eyes on a far-off shoreline.
> Snapshots of the rumpled bed.

I remove pages to bring them on my visits,
coax her into talk with a picture of my sister.

> December 1941 Boston: Carolyn, one week old:
> *There were soldiers with guns on the hospital roof,*
> *blacked-out windows,* my mother says.

Albums shift to color, the family now complete at four.
I bring my father in for today's visit.

> Charlie: annual neighborhood cookout.
> *I made those pink rabbit ears.*

> Charlie: Jackson Falls, bridging two rocks—
> his brown suit, red tie, fedora ... *before he slipped.*

> Charlie: Nahant beach—his red wool bathing suit.
> *Oh, that awful suit that clung.*

And three pages from the last album. How to choose
what might pry a pebble loose from bedrock.

York Harbor: 50th Anniversary Charlie and Polly 1986.
I show the ones dancing. Orchids on her broken wrist. *Oh …*

When I say I can't believe he's been gone twenty years, she nods.
Let's get dressed...he's waiting for us downstairs.

Self-Discipline

I never dot an *i* in a timely way.
I just don't get the point of it.

Everything in me resists
lifting the hand,
the 'coup de plume,'
the relentless rap
of blue-black marks.

Writing the words *hit, strike*,
especially *infuriate*.

A dot should mean one thing. Period.
The end of a sentence. Period.
The end of a marriage. Period.

Food on the Table

My father knew the kindest way
to kill a lobster.
Two fingers spread claws
while the knife draws up
the back with draftsman skill,
cracks the head. I hide
in the kitchen watching
butter clarify.

*

I never tasted fudge quite like his,
dark and sugary,
scored in generous squares.
So why bring up what he withheld?
His heart was his own business.
His hands were open.

*

On Sundays his hands danced
with the honing steel,
a flash and flail precise
as Koussevitzky's beat.
I watched him carve the beef,
each paper-thin slice
a blessing on the family meal
our lives depended on.

At the Nursing Home

In the hallway,
I take out a nectarine.

I bite—
skin, pink-tinged,
breaks,
lips ravished.
Torn flesh
weeps sunlit jewels,
juice running down fingers.
I go deeper
setting teeth
against furrowed pit,
blood red.
I scrape it clean,
until my tongue
tastes wood.
Now, I can return,
palm the doorknob

as if to check
for ripeness.

The Secret

Before I married again,
I asked my father
out to lunch.
Not the safe family unit
with mother along,
just the two of us
to ask his advice.

But really, to find out
who he was,
who he would say
he was.
He didn't.
He said the secret
to a happy marriage
is to give in.
Someone has to win.

Otherwise

Outside Tucson, a sun-flamed cross ignites the desert.
A few miles, and one flashes from the hillside.
Another close to the road with ribbons,
fake flowers, a frizzled teddy bear.

At the fourth, I pull over on rough ground,
fissured by flash floods, scorched air.
But the wood is fragrant, its nails shiny.
Crude letters, *Alina Kathleen Smith—25.*
Laminated photos and notes,
ink still legible, *we miss you.*

I've felt sleep drift in an open window,
past cranked-up music.
I've come up fast on hidden curves.
I've caroused in a crowded car,
looked away laughing.
I've had that argument with traffic.

In an instant it can happen,
full throttle to hush—
a life that otherwise might still be.

White Peony

As if a malevolent cloud
opened up, crazed the terrace,
washed away the topsoil
she loses words and her whereabouts.

Self-seeded and defiant, weeds
insinuate between bricks, unruly,
ragged, up from a taproot
embedded in forgotten soil.

I have regrets…

When she tries to cull daffodils
for conversation, only cut stems
and broken petals remain in her fist.
Still, she arranges a vase for my visit.

I bring a peony to place in a bowl.
From deep creases in its silken bed,
black ants creep one by one,
thrashing in the water, not dying.

I should have done it differently…

She broods over the fragrance,
of this extravagant bloom,
fingers each bruised petal over
and over, as it refuses to yield.

Pantomime

A beetle on his back does not give up on walking.
The desperation is mine.
I turn it over because a being this small
is more legible alive.
Another day, it's my foot that comes down
on the insect, still kicking.
I don't notice because a being this small
is negligible dead.

Hope has this kind of muddle.
One day persisting.
One day perishing.
As we right ourselves.
As we are trampled in the shadow of the boot.
I counted on love up to twelve.
I trusted and married three.
My heart swinging on a rusty hinge still opens.

Harlequin, my hero, slips away
chased by a sinister Pantalone.
Pierrot in pursuit, flapping his wide white pantaloons
knocks me down again.
But when I'm on my back
and you see me still kicking,
know that the desperation is yours.
I'm just rocking myself into another roll in the hay.

Open Mic Night

Frank's Bar is hopping. The piano player rolls out his repertoire,
his hair singed electric yellow in the spotlight. I wait my turn
to sing, wash down panic with beer and banter.

Cigarettes fume on the lips of ashtrays, small pyres pirouette
up my nose, tarnishing any taste for corn chips. I remind myself
no one cares about a dropped jaw, a lifted palate. Instead

I obsess about the text, running over and over the words.
A man grabs his wife for a dance, sings *My Love*
is Here to Stay in her ear and every raspy word stays in mine.

At last, microphone in hand, I brush it to my lips as if I've done
this before, like it wasn't the first time. *Oh it's way past time …*
broadcasts from two speakers on a distant wall.

I want to laugh but something holds me back; perhaps the way
my voice unhooks one strap, falls from its formal training.
The way it prowls, lives the lush life.

III

It's Been a Clear Day

I've seen this blue before —
a cloudless cobalt sky
that may not come again.
I want to take my mother
outside to see. "Is Dad coming?"
she asks about her dead husband.
Most days she asks.

She holds on to my arm
notices shadows
shapes of leaves, flowers,
when suddenly she remembers
nasturtium!
bachelor's button!
Sometimes it comes in a wave!

"What comes?" I ask.
The way I miss him.

The Night Passes Quickly

Because what is
must sleep with the shape of
what is not,
we have moved apart.
    The air pulses with the unsaid.

Thunder moves down river.
Rain, hard, unwinds in waves.
I wake to the down comforter,
a cloud, heavy over me.
    Gone the insensibility of sleep.

Gone the hunger for fault.
I make a space for you to curve
against my back. And now, now
your breath, a flurry,
    your lips unrelenting.

A bluest sky receives us,
drinking coffee beside the beech tree
shedding last night's rain,
its leaves drenched in sun,
lighting our bruised smiles.

The Day My Father Died

I did not let a blizzard stop the tech rehearsal,
and he did not let his wife stop him.

Together we wired paper birds behind the proscenium arch.
White doves to be to be released—
a whoosh-winged awakening for Hansel and Gretel,
lost in a fairyland nightmare.

I never guessed his pain, though thought it strange
he wouldn't climb the ladder to fix a light.
Stranger still, his asking for a hug,
when hesitancy so often held him back.

He said he'd better go, let me scrape the windshield,
as he gripped the steering wheel.
And I never asked, the ice formed so fast,
in whirl-wings of stinging light.

When he spoke again it was in my dream,
Spectral, but whole, rising
from the floor where the medics worked.
Have faith, I hold my shape.

A shoulder of ice slid off my chest—
I let up on the criminal in my keeping.

Late Summer

— a snarl
of red sorrel and crabgrass.
Knotweed under the hosta.
A spindly vine eclipses black-eyed
Susan's last gloomy suns.
I claw through the garden,
cull crabgrass from lilies,
dig out drooping bluebells,
cut back oregano.

Deep in pachysandra,
I burrow in dirt to release
stubborn roots from earth.
I grab, I yank, until my face runs
with grit and tears.
I nip off shriveled heads,
rip vines away from bushes,
reveling in violence.

I Have the Will to Do So

I am animal, a leap,
a tumble, a stride toward sun,
a hurler of stones.
I summon my body
beyond highest branches,
leaf out my will to galaxies,
call myself to act,
carry my daughters to birth.

I am animal, a lag,
a stumble, a curl into shade,
a hunch over cold earth.
I slump in a wheelchair.
But I feel the sun, want to stand
to see the trees. I have the will
to do so. They tell me no.
Who are these two girls I must bear?

My Dead Father Writes to My Dying Mother

Because you will not admit death
kept me from you, I slip
this note under your door.
I fell from grace when you fell
into vacancy. You were sure
I wasn't dead, just buried
in my newspaper, forgetting.

Old letters bundled in your drawer
would tell you everything—
my love undying. But you don't ask
anymore why I'm not there
for dinner, why the nurse
doesn't bring a dahlia for proof
I'm downstairs in the waiting room.

I've become your heart refusing to leave you,
repeating: *sleep now, sleep now, sleep.*

My Father's Annual Stint in the National Guard

He plotted to let his hair down,
sprout a magnificent moustache,
two weeks just long enough apart
from mother, to start a fringe.

Not one whiskering word
in his daily love letters.

It wouldn't be a Fu Manchu droop,
a pencil strip, or, god forbid,
a full beard. Just a small statement,
a once in a while imperial twist.

Instead, his hairs grew hesitant
when they saw her face.
Morsels of food clung.
Kisses, out of the question.

Her ammunition, a steely silence.
His only recourse, the razor.

Defiance washed down the drain,
his gamble for a little hair his own way, dashed.
Evenings he'd raise his martini to a bristling
lip, drink to a lesser god.

Fireworks

An arsenal of antimony and sulfur
packed into shells, ready to sizzle
break apart.

Instead, we talk, damp with caution,
the fight we're having,
a dud.

I want skies lit up, a blaze
of temper, not this black powder
imploded.

Let's heave accusations
with a glitter trail of consequence
that cannot be called back.

Let it sound all night
and let stars break through
when smoke clears.

Sitting for Diego Rivera

—after *Lady in White*, Diego Rivera

Your sable and hog hairs brush my shoulders,
drape a white veil over my head.

How long for you to finish my fingernails? You want me
for mating, for the silk oozing from my body.

And I will smile sweetly, so full of love,
a virgin bride, flushed alizarin.

*

I wait for you, my loom idle,
my lacework done, and you gone.

Each night I pace the halls,
polish my nails. You don't come.

I hold your absence close, mask
the wound of loving, and not having you.

*

Spinnerets flowing, I mend tears,
race silk across spaces. I feel you coming …

Forgive me. It's not my habit
to make a meal of mating,

but you lay there so sweetly,
so dumbly satisfied, and I was still hungry.

My heart is split in two
by loving you   and having you.

You were so mad at me

I didn't know where a walk would take us.
Our unmapped quarrel looked nothing like

a destination. A sun unfiltered by clouds
bore down on us. Jagged peaks bit

into a blue, blue sky. White stones
crunched like oyster shells. Higher

and higher, you took your quickening
breath, pulsing temple, blistered feet.

The path veered into woods to follow
a garrulous stream's twists and turns,

an empty promise of relief. The climb steepened.
Heat brittled, brown-edged grasses.

A buzzing, clacking, whirring
rose around my ankles.

Fluttering insects with their persistent
bicker startled the butterflies.

At the summit of your rage, a breeze rode in
from nowhere, fanning our damp bodies,

our wet hair. Perhaps it was sheer weariness
that took wing with the swallows,

but something ancient appeared before us.
    A ruined chapel, its stone columns

with uneven blocks of light and shadow,
    an open, arched doorway.

Robed in sandstone, dust settling at his feet—
    San Felice, the healer.

IV

Let Me Try to Understand

She doesn't know today
is before tomorrow.
Doesn't know it's she
who gets it wrong after all
these years of being right.

*

If she were coming, she would be here by now.
This means everything to my mother
in her subjunctive mood.
She grabs my arm. *Where were you?*
I'm so glad you're here.

*

She asks for *maroon,*
not the *magenta* sweater,
talks about the *filigree*
of shadows on the wall.

*

Help me! Just this morning
my cat cried out like that
watching a bird,
as if a cat could fly
if only I'd open the window—

that whimper
        of well-fed hunger.

I've seen the nurses bring tissues,
reassure, lean down to talk.

*

It's too much, she says,
but slides in each
cold spoonful, scraping
        the last melt
                of maple walnut.
We drive back over the Charles,
the river hardly moving

kayaks skimming
        red and yellow
                red and yellow
our car window open
our hair blown free.
It's been just an hour.
                Oh no,
look where we are — that place!

*

Lipstick on her eyebrows.
I let it pain me,
as if I had a stone in my shoe.

*

Shingles scalds her forehead
    shutting one eye.
It's an old nerve harboring a grudge
its venom unleashed
    now that there's a break
in her defense.

*

Today she tells me
they spray her leftovers
before they feed the goats.
What goats?
    The ones in the basement,
she smiles, but insists,
hours alone until now   upright
in her brown fabric chair.

*

She will not take her pills
clamps her mouth—
Will not!

The nurse's trump
a contraption
like a garlic press
to pulverize.

We spoon bitter
applesauce in.

*

In lapses she remains
as she was,
    an eager stab at her Jell-O
    the careful wipe
    her white napkin red with parted lips.

The upper lip   twin mounds
the lower   a tapered wing
each lip print fading
    a flock of doves
    disappearing.

The Road Was Narrow

No soft shoulders, no breakdown lane,
tree trunks drumming by. Row
after row of writhen sunflowers,
crickets shrill ascending.

Spain, and we're still arguing,
the air, a hundred and ten, the road,
one lane, a surgeon's cut through farmlands,
fuel gauge edging empty.

You stop the car, grab
your pack from the back seat
to walk the parched way we came,
becoming small, smaller.

I could have left you then,
driven on to Parador de Carmona,
its cool porcelain, blue, gold and white,
instead of bursting into flame.

Invictus Inverted

I accelerate to pass an 18-wheeler,
as my foot inches toward the brake.
Will I speed by—a quick glance

in the rear-view at what I've left?
Or panic as I hit the blinker,
slink back behind the truck?

Migrating monarchs don't hesitate,
orange and black confetti against blue.
No flustering at a crossroads,

choosing to do or die, and
twenty million will, by windshields
or weakness, be wiped out.

They don't worry if they'll survive
to weigh down the oyamel fir
or if a bough might break.

I'm done with mastering my fate.
Let blue sky come up to my ankles,
with the empiricism of monarchs.

Breeze lift, sun guide, earth pull.
High noon devours shadow. I am
outside consequence of will,

neither headstrong nor hesitant.
Let each branch have sway
with the wind. I cling.

Pastorales Tahitiennes

— after Paul Gaugin

The tree will not reveal itself
roots clutch the ground
leaves remain staunchly green.

Look long, and words go
yellow vibrates
a pipe tune wrestles
shadows from the ground

buds burst pink smoke
orange flames
a rock opens a saffron eye.

Look long enough.
In twilight, milkweed voltaic,
a river's black throat echoes

Virgin and Vermillion gods
in their dusky pleasure.

Packing

Mornings arrive sweet with smell of wood pulp—
boxes flattened. We talk divisions:

the Picasso print, a coin toss,
the rooster napkin-holder from Portugal stays.

Majorca tiles are wrapped, one to each.
Other souvenirs, tossed in the trash.

You keep a knife sharp so the cut can be clean,
scoring and bending cardboard for holding in.

Your belongings, sealed and labeled,
stacked into a dark interior, you muscle

through the silence, while I, as usual, spill
enough words for both of us, but not to you.

Left alone, my feet no longer tiptoe the floors
and room after room opens up.

On the Scent of a Tune

Can you name it … this scent
rising from the piano?

If I put my nose into it,
it doesn't knock me out like Tchaikovsky,

with his rose parade, or pepper
my sinuses like a Bach toccata.

I first noticed the scent of music
at the outdoor stadium in Verona,

hand-held candles burning down
to the down beat, a darkening sky.

The first whiff of a Puccini opera,
then bar after bar of milk chocolate.

I couldn't stop, not even in church,
when Poulenc let out a thunderous fart,

his fine art of colliding harmonies.
At night street corners smoked

with electrical fire—Cybotron and Wire
wannabes burning up the beat.

To this day I can't smell incense
without a Gregorian chant

flaring my nostrils.
And licorice, I hate it.

It reeks like the Muzak
secreting from every mall.

But this riff is elusive, a jig
that stirs up Jambalaya, or a sprig,

some species of ambrosia,
unpacked and aired out tonight,

to tickle the nostrils,
arouse the feet. Ragtime!

The Lure

Snagged in the curtain,
your fishing lure, unnoticed
until it pricks my finger,
a delicate deception.

It's worth this small agony—
the unexpected irony
that you left
this behind.

A cross between a minnow
and elongated bumblebee.
Scales, cross-hatched,
down the back in fine bands.

A decoy, itself caught—
unseeing black pupils,
yellow eyes, perfectly round.
A silver heart at its lip.

From its underbelly, smudged red,
two hooks hang like chandeliers,
arched barbs in each prong.
One tip lodged in my thumb.

Unlike its intended victim,
I have another hand to pull it out,
before the limpid line becomes taut,
before I fight back and flesh rips.

I extract. I extricate myself.
    From the line I untangle,
    a lead weight
    slides off into my hand.

Reckoning

Magnifying the saw-tooth edge
    on a blade of grass, an ant's bulbous belly,
below the bifocal line. My lost glasses.

I retrace the way I've been, eyes on weeds
    off the path, looking for a metal frame glinting,
a sidewise glance. I don't give up easily.

Things must take up space, so to all lost, things a place!
    Blue sweater behind the chair; under a newspaper, the keys;
umbrellas just about everywhere. Some to forfeit, some to find.

I tell myself—*Of course, they can be replaced!* These,
    with another pair, a sweater in a warmer shade.
A lover who won't misplace what I say. I tried my best.

Words can be tossed out, lost to interpretation. Look
    how I go back over the same ground,
trying to retrieve what I said. Without the dash of it.

And what's left if I can't retract or replace?
    Loss, that's it, isn't it? A thing in itself.

Miniature Persimmon, Dark Orange

Pulp torn from rind, pale
seeds I swallow whole,
my fingers stained.

My father's office, empty.
Gone his squares and angles,
his mechanical pencils in the glass kitchen jar.
His cube eraser, effaced.

No drawing of Ayer High School
laid out, the lean of his lettering,
the little arcs to indicate
where one could leave
and not come back.

Letter to Myself Unremembered

By the time you receive this,
you will not remember me,
but see this bedside letter for the first
time every day. Whoever Diana is.

You knew once it could happen,
turning a page, losing the story,
staring at tiles on your scrabble rack,
not able to find the right word.

Let me tell you, you were clever
exchanging low count letters
for a chance at luck, saving the *Q*
in case you drew the *U*. Now,

just vowels, and fear without a name.
And I, I don't think of you anymore.

V

Between Selves

My lips brushed the pillow.
I felt my body, its changing landscape.

Moss grew in crevices.
Buds swelled, petals opened.

Dry riverbeds for ivory streams,
blood in the bayou.

The sky existed for stellar collisions,
I existed to be touched.

No one knew I hid in the cedar closet,
the comforter under me.

What I discovered all by myself,
hips lifting, lips clamped shut.

Everything physical mattered.
Smiles practiced in store windows.

My body in tight sweaters.
Its effusion, its fragrance.

Going steady, stir-crazy, going stupid.
Writing down what I'd say

when Jimmy calls, his ring on a chain
around my neck. My parents laughing.

When he squeezed my shoulder
at the movies, I froze, afraid he'd kiss me.

Afraid he wouldn't. So much for Junior High.
The rest erased, a reddening in its wake.

I was between selves, but even today,
although I have a steady hand,

when soldering stained glass,
a feather-white to cobalt blue,

I surge with the silver along each seam
as it melts under a hot iron.

The Day My Mother Dies

I don't cancel. I want the sting
of the dentist needle, deadened senses.

I let him dig around, my mouth agape,
eyes shut against the glaring lamp.

I hear the whirr, feel the fray
of tooth touch my lip;

let the taps, clinks do their job—
a hole prepared with smooth sides.

Then feel without pain the hole
slowly filled, the tamping down

the tuck and scrape of amalgam.
How carefully my dentist works

to smooth the surface.
His work is a blessing,

its small precision
sensations I can manage.

I Own This

I have run with bulls
been gored
tasted the granularity of earth.
Stood up.
My face wet
heart illuminated,
wept the garden back to life.

Looking Hard at What You See

—after *Still Life*, Giorgio Morandi

I am going to simplify my life,
wear muted clothes, brown skirts
and white shirts, sensible shoes,
a gray hat.

Who wouldn't want to be that
humble in harmony with those
leaning in to touch another
quietly

and experience how supple
an edge can be. How shadow
suggests the rounding out
of surface.

To be both squared and solid,
containing the salt of the earth
and a vessel to keep oil ready
to pour.

I don't need to stand out
in red heels or consider if purple
earrings go with a pink
pencil skirt,

always the painted lady
running errands in bright sun.
I had my heyday, now
I must blend in,

rest, welcome a diffused
light, the illusion of space,
with no need to move through it.
To be still,

allow dust to accumulate on lips,
permit myself to float free
of the shelf, the table and become
a pure geometry.

Closure

It fell into my yard, but missed the porch.
A main branch, a mother lode of sap rot.

This limb, which each spring bloomed
toward my window to divert me

as I wrote, gives up its camouflage,
leaves still in tight buds

that will not fan out, seeds
that won't helicopter down.

It lies on the lawn, a wreckage,
wrenched from heartwood.

*

This branch is not first to fall
under the weight of a late snow,

not the first that gave in to a winter gale,
a temper that rasped and split.

Stubs mark breaking points
where wounds sealed off.

The tree, so empty now, power lines racing
through its middle without resistance.

I write starkly without distraction.
Go, grieve, forgive.

A Day Like No Other

The park
bristles sunlight,
green leaves
as vibrant filters.
On the pond's surface
filaments and spores
flash above gold rocks.
Wings skitter back
and forth, voltaic.
A plane gleams
trailing two white ribbons.

*

The lake
clings to the Labrador,
streams
like a waterfall
from her belly.
Eyes closed
she shudders,
fur flailing,
lost in a corona mist.

*

Walking out
of tree shadows,
a man sings.
On his shoulders
a child, legs swinging,
their two heads close
as a totem, each edged
in the nimbus of back light
bestowed on saints.

Refrain

Sparrow churrs inside the chimney.
A leaf that won't let go.
Salmon frozen in the waterfall.

What takes the fish upstream?
What takes the sparrow down?

Sudden wind stalls the arrow.
Stillness bends the bow.
No one stands beneath the bough.

What keeps the arrow fastened?
What makes the leaf let go?

Trees palsied in the orchard
Where apples never grow.
A plow buried deep in snow.

What keeps the soil unseeded?
What makes the blossoms close?

My father died too quickly.
My mother died too slow.
Sorrow frozen in the long ago.

What sets the sparrow flying?
The arrow, letting go?

Nik Wallenda Walks a Wire across Niagara Falls

Into a theater of wind and mist
a cable dips, disappears.

He moves steadily,
each step shortening
the improbable.
He dissolves into thunder.

The camera loses   then finds his face
soaked, focused
on distance relenting.

In shoes his mother made,
elk-skin suede
his feet curl along the wire.

He tells the cameraman
his arms are numb.
Weighs the long pole
in sighs, side to side.

And we can see
the waters waiting
the letting go
the urge to.

He inches ahead
each second of inertia
a pinpoint
from which we too
step forward.

What You Make of It

—after the photograph, *Winter Ice,* Alyson McCann

What I've wrung out of love
is not one steady course

but a dozen starts,
a dozen frangible ends

sprawled on the windowpane,
a wild white tumbleweed.

Flexing and bending,
I made love fast

past the break of day,
stubbing out my cigarette

to begin again. Each tried
direction seemed right.

My feathers, frilly and feminine,
fletched to the will of those I wanted.

I felt it all, each spiral turn,
each layback spin

in the dark, despite the dark.
I take nothing back.

The sun has reached the day I'm in.

www.ingramcontent.com/pod-product-compliance
Lightning Source LLC
Chambersburg PA
CBHW022201160726
48282CB00024B/270

* 9 7 8 8 1 9 6 2 0 2 6 9 9 *